A DECADE IN RHODESIA

A DECADE IN RHODESIA

Alice Elsie Bell

ATHENA PRESS
LONDON

ISBN 1 84401 472 X

First Published 2005
ATHENA PRESS
Queen's House, 2 Holly Road
Twickenham TW1 4EG
United Kingdom

Printed for Athena Press

Dedication

I dedicate this book to my deceased parents, John and Eva Alice Bell, who were the 'Best of British', and my siblings, Dorothy Marlene, Wendy, Rodney and Sandra Jane, without whom this book would never have been written.

My thanks also to our extended family, the Native employees on both Yale and Oxford farms, who made life in Rhodesia so worthwhile and enjoyable.

Also a very big thanks to the ladies of Neithrop and Banbury libraries, North Oxfordshire, England, for all their help and use of computers over the year 2004.

Mum and Dad, you would have loved this little book. I miss you, Alice.

To everybody who encouraged me along the way, thank you.

Author's Foreword

This is a true story about a young English family of six, leaving post war Britain for the colonies, Southern Rhodesia, Africa, in the 1950s.

After a couple of years' easy living at Little England Estates, owned by Sir Dennistoun Burney and frequented by the then governor General of Rhodesia, Sir John Nobel Kennedy, the Bell family then bought a couple of farms, in particular Yale and Oxford, which were virgin land in every way!

Then began a way of life that can only be described as hard work and lots of fun, filled with human frailties and insight into the way of life in a hot, basic country with few mod cons.

The ten years produced two well established, mixed farms, which started with the family literally making their own bricks for their home and other buildings.

The farms provided jobs and homes for over a hundred natives and their families and were the base of the Bell clan's background for years to come.

Contents

The Cape Town Castle *Liner*

Built: 1938 by Harland & Wolff, Belfast
Tonnage: 27,000g, 16,454n
Engine: Twin Screw, 2 x 10 Cylinder
Burmeister & Wain 4,650 NHP, 28,000 BHP,
22.5 Knots
Passengers: 290 First-class, 500 Cabins
Launched: 23rd September 1937, completed 31st
march 1938

The *Cape Town Castle* was launched by Mrs JD Low, Mayoress of Cape Town, and the ship's title, along with all other south African castles, was fictional. She continued on the mail service until being taken over for use as a troopship in 1940, and in 1943 she transported American Servicemen from the States to the UK. During the build up to D-Day the *Cape Town Castle* was codenamed Operation Bolero. Released back to Union Castle in 1946, she underwent extensive refurbishment at Belfast and resumed the mail run once more with accommodation for 243 First-class, 553 Tourist-class passengers.

Across the Line

The *Cape Town Castle* liner sailed slowly and gently away from the quayside at Southampton docks, at four o'clock on Thursday 20th July 1949, taking with her the weekly mail to Cape Town, South Africa, and two hundred first-class plus four hundred and sixty-five second-class passengers.

There was a large crowd of excited people with mixed feelings, waving goodbye to post-war Britain; but apprehensive about the life ahead in what was for most a foreign country, Africa!

Eva Alice Bell and her four children, Dorothy Marlene, eleven years old; Alice Elsie, eight years; Wendy, six years; and Rodney, four years, gathered close together, waving to the faint shapes on the quayside far below the liner.

The *Cape Town Castle* was one of the Union Castle liners which had been taking post-war mail to Cape Town since 1938. The liners soon became popular with the public not only for business trips to and from each destination, but as an enjoyable two-week holiday.

The only port of call on the major route was Madeira, but no disembarkation was allowed. However, much to the delight of the passengers, native children provided great entertainment by diving from their small boats for coins thrown from the ship. Many adults clambered aboard with their wares to sell, which were an assortment of lace cloths and pretty clothes.

Then it was a slow, steady sail of 2,500 nautical miles to Cape Town, crossing the equator on the seventh day. There were two passengers to a cabin, with outside portholes: Mum and Rodney in one; Wendy and Alice in another; Dorothy with one to herself. It was a lovely ship, with entertainment and games rooms for the toddlers, a swimming pool and deck games for the older children, and fancy dress for all.

We four children were quite enthralled, but poor Mum, a day or two after leaving Madeira, started to feel quite seasick. She spent a lot of time in her cabin and often the nurse had to appear and administer seasick pills, which just seemed to make her worse! We were quite alarmed when she was retching only bile and was as white as a sheet.

Dorothy, when not with either Mum or Rodney, spent most of her time beside the pool reading a book from the ship's extensive library.

Crossing the equator was an event in itself; with the arrival of King Neptune, the festivities began. The passengers who were willing – and there were plenty – were covered from head to toe in a swill of flour, eggs and milk! The ship was then halted in its voyage and someone jumped, or was thrown, overboard! Everybody else was ducked in the swimming pool. It was very hot, and so everybody stayed in the pool for as long as possible. It was quite a memorable occasion that stayed with us children for some time after.

Some days the sailing got quite rough and the dining room became half empty. After three days of very rough sailing one elderly lady died. Whilst we (the ones able to eat meals) were at breakfast, she was sewn into a muslin bag and slid over board, with a few words read from the Bible.

We were very alarmed after this 'burial at sea' because Mum got worse and worse, and never ever came to the dining room for meals. We knew the doctor and nurse attending her were very worried, but nothing short of stopping the boat would bring an end to her misery. The nurse got Mum to sit in a deck chair in the cool of the evening on the upper deck, where she appeared to get some relief.

Three nuns always sat on the chairs on the upper deck every evening, and we wondered if they ever went to their cabins to sleep, as they were always in the same chairs! We children used to spend some time talking to them, and Wendy said how contented they looked; Dorothy said she wanted to be like them when she grew up! A nun!

Rodney took great advantage of his partial freedom, and was most of the time in the toddlers' playroom, playing with the Meccano set, like the one he had left behind in Dorset.

The last night on board was marked by a fancy dress parade, which everyone joined in. Dorothy went as Mary Poppins, with a wide, colourful skirt and a tight belt, which gave her real style. Alice went as a rainbow, with layers of different coloured paper wrapped around her and a gold ruffle on her head. Wendy went as a sun goddess, all in yellow, with a wand and gold slippers; she looked dazzling. Rodney went as

Dennis the Menace so didn't have to look any different than usual!

A lady dressed as a basket of fruit won; she looked very uncomfortable, but colourful.

Even Mum came down to watch the event and clapped as we walked the circuit. It was a fun event.

It was a lovely end to an eleven-day sea voyage; but it was a very relieved Mother who stepped down the gang plank, with her four children, early that August morning 1949 onto the beautiful harbour of Cape Town.

Overland

The overland train was already in the Cape Town station waiting to depart, later that afternoon, for Rhodesia 1,500 miles away, the landlocked country of our choice.

Dad had already shown us (before he had left, six months in advance) lovely brochures of our new schools, the pupils all in white with white straw hats on their heads and tennis rackets in their hands.

The sun was shining; so different to the grey clouds and grey clothes of England.

Dad had gone on ahead to Gwebe Agricultural College, near the capital, Salisbury, to learn how to grow tobacco, and as he was a teacher of agriculture he could teach others.

It was a long trip on the train, through the Great Karroo Desert, which was spectacular. To wake up early in the morning, lift up the blinds on the window and see the wide expanse of desert scrubs, and watch the magnificent sun rise was quite beautiful.

We knew then that we were going to love this wild, untamed country, come what may!

Daylight bought us speeding onto Kimberley, famous for diamonds and the Big Hole, on the Orange Free State border.

It was starting to feel very hot, and stops en route were a welcome distraction, which allowed us children to lower, the windows, lean out for more air and see what the natives were trying to sell.

Wendy was much intrigued by the piccanins' curly hair, and stretched out her hand to touch one small, tightly curled head. She got the fright of her life when a monkey the piccanin was holding jumped up and bit her finger. It was a nasty bite, with lots of blood and screaming from us all. Mum had to rush Wendy to the conductor, who treated the bleeding finger with a good scrub, smeared it with antibiotic cream and wrapped it round with a bandage.

This unexpected, painful event dampened our enthusiasm somewhat, making us keep our hands to ourselves and inside the train!

The train sped on to Mafeking, crossing into Botswana through the edge of another desert, the Kalahari, which was just as sparse as the Great Karroo, with that empty beauty and stillness.

We arrived at Francis Town, on the border of Southern Rhodesia, the next night, crossing the Limpopo River. After a few hours in customs clearance offices, we went on to Plumtree, a quite sedate looking town; then onto the railway junction at Bulawayo, the second biggest town in Southern Rhodesia.

The countryside had changed drastically en route, from dry scrubland with sightings of warthogs with plenty of babies running around and grotesque baobab trees to savannah grasslands and kopies, with strange, beautiful rocks.

We had a couple of hours to waste in Bulawayo, so we all walked into the wide main street running through the centre of the town. Having lunch at a nearby café, we were told by the owner that all the streets in Bulawayo had to be 'wide enough to turn a span of oxen', hence the lovely wide roads, lined with jacaranda trees with their blue flowers and hard, scented wood. These trees were introduced to Africa from Southern America in the nineteenth century, and had adapted so well one would have thought they were indigenous!

The last part of the journey, of about three hundred and sixty miles, took us through half the length of the country, virtually in a straight line, passing the towns of Gwelo, Gatooma, Hartley, then at last to our destination, the capital of Southern Rhodesia, Salisbury.

It was mid afternoon when the train pulled into Salisbury, and quite a crowd were gathered on the platform to welcome the weary travellers.

Rodney was the first to spy Dad, which wasn't hard, as he stood head and shoulders above everybody else; at six foot three he was easy to find in the welcoming throng.

Little England Estates, 1950

Back row, right to left: John Bell (Dad) Sir Dennistoun Burney, Eva Alice Bell (Mum), Lady Kennedy, Sir John Noble Kennedy, accountant, and his wife, Lady Burney.
Front row, right to left: Alice Elsie Bell, Rodney Bell, Wendy Bell, Dorothy Marlene Bell

S alisbury, the capital of Southern Rhodesia, is approximately 5,500 feet above sea level, with a very pleasant climate all the year round. It has interesting, attractive shops and markets where both natives and white people seemed to mix harmoniously together.

After a joyful reunion with Dad we were all excited to see our new home; Dad first of all insisted on Mum buying us each a mosquito net for our beds, and a large quantity of quinine tablets.

Then came the exciting part of climbing onto the back of the Ford pickup truck for the journey of twenty miles to Little England Estates; and so home. Dad, Mum and Dorothy sat inside the pickup truck (Dorothy refused to sit in the back – ever) and the rest of us climbed in the back with the cases. We loved it, with the wind in our hair, holding on for dear life!

Little England Estates was a large, well run farming enterprise belonging to Baronet and Lady Dennistoun Burney. Dad was introducing tobacco to the estate, plus supervising other farming aspects as well as building Sir Dennistoun Burney a huge house made out of local stone.

The Estate was a lovely area to live in, surrounded by indigenous mapani trees, which were alive with all sorts of wildlife.

The wood pigeons woke us all up in the mornings with their *too-wit-twoo*, and at night the crickets started in full swing as soon as it became dark, which was usually seven o'clock.

Dad was in his element and would be off at the crack of dawn on his horse, often taking Dorothy with him. They both loved to ride in the wide open spaces.

We had two native servants in the house, and two in the garden. As the veranda went right around the house, a lot of one of the servant's time was spent putting red polish on and shining it up like mad!

Mum and Dad had a lot of entertaining to do, as the Governor General of Southern Rhodesia, Sir John Noble Kennedy, and his

Wendy and Alice, Little England Estates, 1950

wife, Lady Kennedy, were often at our home. They were big friends of Sir Dennistoun Burney, and very interested in the farming aspect and running of the Estate.

Lady Kennedy was very kind to Mum and often took her back with her to Government House to stay whilst we children were at boarding school. Mum missed us dreadfully, and missed Dorset just as much. Africa to her was a man's country.

There were two white farm assistants on the Estate, Mr Tatham and Mr Popperwell; also a native bookkeeper, with a very smart office, who used to ask Alice what she was going to do when she grew up. 'A bookkeeper, with a neat office like yours,' she would reply.

One morning we went to Mr Popperwell's house and he was busy on his corrugated roof, nailing it down, when an amazing thing happened. A huge whirlwind sprang up and lifted the corrugated roof, with Mr Popperwell on it, clean into the air and away! Like a magic carpet, the corrugated sheet glided along in the wind with an excited, frightened Mr Popperwell in a very nervous state. We three children were enthralled; it was all so sudden, and spectacular to watch!

One evening, Dad called us children, in great excitement, to come and look. Outside, right across the sky, was a wonderful sight; the sun was setting and a great big ball of fire, all red and yellow, filled the horizon. We watched until the spectacle slowly disappeared. It was a sight unequalled by anything we had seen before in our short lives. It was marvellous; the picture poets and artists would die for.

We still had to do our bit in the garden, even with two garden boys. It didn't take us long to realise that digging with a trowel was hard work, and most ineffective in the hard, dry African earth. We soon transferred to *badzas*, like the natives used. You just had to watch your feet though, and not chop yours or your neighbour's toes off, as Rodney nearly did! Too heavy work for a young lad, perhaps…

The cool of the evenings was the time everybody liked best, especially the natives, when Dad would put up four football posts, and from nowhere and everywhere a horde of people would appear, both young and old, and a game of football would commence.

The natives loved it. Rodney would be the only white boy, with Dad on the sidelines with the whistle.

Wendy and Alice begged to join in, but it was strictly boys only and they were not allowed, so they just stood on the sidelines, cheering them on with the other girls.

It was great fun, and enjoyed by all.

This sport would take place two or sometimes three times a week; but never on a Friday evening, as the African beer would have been brewing all day, ready for the big

Friday party. By nightfall the tom-toms would start drumming, *bum, bum, bum*, then the dancing would begin; a steady, heavy *thump, thump, thump*, with loud cries, right up into the sky.

This would go on for hours; round and round in a circle the natives would go, thumping with their bare feet; men, women and children, dancing, jumping, leaping and falling about; and drinking strong, homemade maize beer.

The cries would go on well into the early hours, getting weaker and weaker, until nearly the break of day. Then a great hush would descend.

An hour later the wood pigeons would start, *varoo, varoo*; and a cool, beautiful morning would awake; then Dad would be out on his horse to greet the dawning day.

Dad always had a dog, and the dog was always, but always called Bob, so here in Africa Dad had his 'big bad dog, Bob'; always a mongrel and always good tempered.

Little England Estates

Little England Estates

Mum, Dad and Rodney

Dad and Bob

Ticks were a big nuisance to the way of life in the tropics, and being a parasite they clung onto any being with blood to suck. Cattle and dogs were easy prey, so us children were, from day one, shown how to clear the dogs each day of these horrible little creatures.

The big fat grey ones were easy to see, remove and drop into a jam jar that had a mixture of water and antiseptic inside. The tiny flat brown and striped ones were much more difficult to see and remove, and one had to be careful that one removed the head, as it usually appeared to be stuck in the body of the host. Yucky!

Apparently it was the small, flat tick that gave the deadly illness to dogs called biliary, which made the animal loose weight and eventually die. Humans could contract tick fever from these bites, and the effect was horrendous; terrible headaches and sometimes death.

The fat grey ticks could become purple with gorged blood and usually fell off themselves, but it was the delight of us younger children to pull them off (there were plenty of them every day) and pop them; blood would shoot right up into the air, hitting everyone and everything in sight, dark red blood!

There were usually a couple of other dogs as well as Bob. Mum had one, a little white and black terrier called Timmy. An alarming thing happened to Timmy; he started running round in circles, barking like mad. Mum tried to calm him down by cuddling him; but this seemed to make him more frantic! His eyes started rolling around and he tried to bite Mum. She put him in a spare bedroom where he seemed to go completely mad, growling, jumping in the air; then, worst of all, foaming at the mouth.

It was quite scary to watch.

Mum, bless her, decided, to take Timmy a bowl of water just as Dad walked into the house. Dad took one look at Timmy, grabbed Mum by the scruff of the neck, and literary threw her across the passage away from the foaming terrier!

He then went and got a gun and shot Timmy dead. It was devastating and shocking, as it all happened so fast. Yes, poor Timmy had rabies; deadly and lethal.

Little England Estate was the perfect place to start life in Rhodesia as it was decidedly 'up market' and safe compared to the 'great outside'.

Apart from mosquitoes, ticks, rabies, whirlwinds and heat, Little England Estate was heaven! Who knew what was out there?

One incident, which gave Alice a clue to colonial rule, was when Sir Dennistoun Burney and Dad asked her to tell the 'boys,' at the back of the house to come around to the veranda at the front.

Alice went to the 'boys', and at nine years old was momentary stumped on how to address these adult natives, three feet taller than her! She could see that colonial rule was going to be another way of life!

So, on to the next adventure...

Pater

Boarding School

Rodney, Wendy (Norton Junior School),
Dorothy Marlene (Queen Elizabeth High),
Alice Elsie (Norton Junior School)

Boarding schools in Rhodesia must not be confused with boarding schools in England, where usually only the elite and wealthy can afford to send their children. Because most people lived so far from towns or the nearest schools in Rhodesia boarding schools were a must from a very early age.

Even so, the cost of boarding must have been astronomical for Pater, as he never stopped moaning about the fees; prompting a reactionary statement from Dorothy, 'Well, we never asked to be born!' True!

Dorothy, being twelve years old, went straight to Queen Elizabeth High School for girls in Salisbury, but as Dorothy pointed out, it was not as 'up market' as the school she expected to go to in Sherborne back home in Dorset.

Even so, it was the best of schools, where the Prime Minister's daughter, Judith Todd, was a pupil when Alice and Wendy attended. In 1980 it was renamed after Robert Mugabe's late wife as 'Sally Mugabe High School' for girls; and, no doubt quite rightly, it is now filled with a different colour of children.

The rest of us younger children went off to the country school 'Norton Junior School', which was about twenty-eight miles south of Salisbury. Norton was a farming area, and the school an old British

Air Force base. The same buildings still stood and so were used not much differently by the school. The barracks, used as hostels, were given aircraft names. Wendy and Alice were in De Havilland House, and Rodney in Lancaster.

Mr Hall, the headmaster, was there as long as we were; in fact, after we left the school was renamed after him – Dudley Hall – and he went on to become a school inspector.

Mr Hall was a big, jovial, very pleasant man, who was everybody's father; so different to our strict Pater who believed that children should always be busy, working or even just reading, but never, never idle. He ran the school like an army camp; everything on time and in order. He was aware of each child by name and seemed to be in control of everything.

Mr Hall had what he thought was a treat for us boarders who were unlucky enough to have reached a birthday. He would enter the hostel first thing in the morning, whilst everyone was still asleep in bed. Then the unlucky birthday girl or boy would be lifted clean out of their beds by arms and legs and unceremoniously bumped on the hostel floor for however many years of age had been reached.

It was an extremely painful procedure; apart from the screams of pain, which Mr Hall obliviously took for joy, the child was inevitably left in bruised and often crying state.

No one complained as there was no one to complain to, so we just took it as part of boarding school life and were just glad we only had one birthday a year!

Being an old Air Force base, the runway went off in an overgrown, derelict state, with an assortment of underground tunnels, which the school children soon discovered, and many hours were spent exploring the passages.

The school, of course, was under the English Educational System, and the three Rs were taught, with much emphasis on

English history, which Alice enjoyed thoroughly and excelled at.

Being a pleasant climate, sport was a big part of the school curriculum, and whilst the girls enjoyed many hours of tennis, Rodney was into football and rounders. Everybody played netball, boys and girls. Swimming, of course, was the main sport in all Rhodesian schools, and everybody, just everybody, swam nearly every day. So all in all it was a healthy way of life, but sadly there is usually a dark side to an otherwise rosy life.

There was a hospital in the school grounds which was run by the matron/sister called Mrs MacDonald. Wendy used to go fairly regular for a dose of malt and cod-liver oil, which she enjoyed. Wendy tended to be very thin and weak, but blessed with the brains of the family, and later the looks.

One does not like to dwell on the negatives in life, but the damage caused by evil was and is very profound. There was a doctor living in the school grounds who was obviously in charge of the local hospital, which would have attended to both the school and the community. Alice had to be seen by this doctor for stomach ache and was put in a far end ward by the matron. There the doctor proceeded to sexually abuse her whilst sitting on a chair at the end of the high hospital bed. He told Alice to hold onto the railings at the top, and not to scream too loudly. Alice was ten years old and did as she was told. It was extremely sore, and seemed to go on forever. Why didn't the matron come in? One realises much later on in life that the doctor must have been masturbating himself.

Alice told no one about this abuse, but would not go near the hospital again. Many, many years later, Wendy and Alice were discussing this and Wendy said that something similar had happened to her with the same doctor, but Wendy, though younger, was wiser and reported it to a matron at the hostel who reported it to the headmaster. Goodness knows how many children this doctor had abused, with, I am sure, the knowledge of the hospital matron, Mrs MacDonald. Terrible, terrible.

Before I began writing this story, a request was made of the school for information about the hostel names, and also the name of the doctor at that time, but no answer was received.

Norton School was famous for the starting up of a Young Farmers' Club and was publicly proclaimed in the local and national newspaper for all its achievements. One of the main projects was the growing of vegetables for the school kitchen, and Alice was given an award for her large and rosy tomatoes. Photos of Alice and her enormous tomatoes went down in the school reference books, and many, many years later, her nephews going to the same school recognised their aunty Alice by her fat plaits, freckled face and big tomatoes!

Every Saturday night the school showed a film, which a lot of the village people also attended. Those days the cowboy films were at a premium and Alice fell madly in love with the cowboy Roy Rogers, completely ignoring Dale Evans, his wife, and insisted he was going to come for her on Trigger, his horse!

Alice would wait at the school gate for what seemed hours, even missing her meals, until the headmaster sent a teacher to bring her inside and explain to Alice that Roy Rogers wouldn't be coming because he was married to Dale Evans. Was Roy Rogers just a lifeline from the drama of real life?

The cowboy films had a carry-on effect for the smitten watchers, and many an afternoon playtime was spent reliving cowboys and Indians. Reins were made from the monkey rope pulled from the trees and tied around a boy, who was then the horse! Branches of leaves were wound around the other boys' and girls' heads, and they were then the Indians. A lot of running around and chasing went on, and it was a favourite afternoon game for all.

It is always said that a child has a favourite teacher, but Alice seemed to fall foul of the Standard Four teacher Mr Sanders, an ex-squadron leader, who insisted on being called Sir, and flicked short stubs of chalk at pupils' heads, specially at their ears, with an expert aim. He must have bought many German planes down with his expertise!

Rodney, at five years old, found it hard to settle down at boarding school, and even though Alice and Wendy went to his hostel each night to kiss him goodnight and in winter to put Vaseline on the back of his hands to keep him from getting chapped, he was a lost little soul.

Rodney ran away from Norton School twice, following the railway line to Salisbury. He had a tiny square case, which he filled each time with cornflakes, sugar and milk, at breakfast time, for his journey. The milk warped the case. Each time the police picked him up and telephoned the parents at Little England Estates. Poor soul never got very far, but it seemed to Rodney a great escape!

Mum was devastated, and no matter how much she begged to keep him at home, to teach him herself, Dad would not relent. One feels that with the loss of the first son, Arnold, from diphtheria at three years old, Dad's heart was buried with him in that tiny grave.

Mum and Dad's world collapsed the year of Arnold's death – June 1941 – and things were never quite the same again, hence the move to Dorset, then later on to Africa, but one's losses go with one.

One exciting event took place whilst Alice, Wendy and Rodney were pupils at Norton School; the King and Queen of England came to Rhodesia on a visit.

The royals were doing a tour of Rhodesia on the Blue train, which was going to pass through the village of Norton at 5.30 a.m.! Consequently, there was a whole school of little children lining the railway that early morning for a glimpse of their monarch.

Yes, bless her, Queen Elizabeth, fully dressed with her lovely hat on, stood in full view of the window, waving to the horde of cheering children holding Union Jack flags. It was a special event for the schoolchildren of the commonwealth, which they didn't forget.

Norton school was recognised as a model and excellent primary school, but like all institutions, everything depended on the structure of the people in charge, and one predator in the midst can cause untold and long lasting effect. Goodness knows how that doctor got to be in that position of trust in the first place.

Even so, we are sure Norton School, which is now Dudley Hall Junior School, is still a school of excellence and popular with the public far and wide.

We still feel, as children of boarding schools, that they are not appropriate for small children of primary school age. Senior school, maybe; but that's our opinion, Alice, Wendy and Rodney Bell.

Sunnybank Farm

Sunnybank Farm, Golden Valley, Gatooma

Dad went into partnership with a Mr Harden and bought Sunnybank Farm in the Golden Valley district of Gatooma.

Golden Valley was primarily a mining area and well known mega-companies like Rio Tinto were mining gold and ore and paying the natives low wages for their labour.

Sunnybank Farm had its good and very bad points; unfortunately the latter were dominant.

There was a lovely flourishing garden at the back of the house, still very colourful when we move in, where we always took our afternoon tea. The mulberry trees were well established and stood in a long line. They were so profuse that they intertwined and made a wonderful tree house and playground for us younger children. What with eating the mulberries, which were delicious and plentiful, our mouths were always stained purple from their juice.

It wasn't only us children who ate the mulberries; Mum made many tasty mulberry pies; she also found us some silk worms, which feed on the mulberry leaves. Then the little busy worms spun 1,500 metres of silk (about a mile), before disappearing into a cocoon, later on eating their way out to become a moth, lay their eggs and then die. Wonderful procedure!

We don't know how old the farm was, but it must at one time have been an extensive tobacco farm, because the tobacco barns were large and very old. So old, that one day, whilst having afternoon tea in the pretty rear garden, there was a terrific bang, thud and clouds of dust and smoke covered us all. The whole structure of barns had collapsed. It was amazing, just lucky we were not growing Virginia Tobacco! Goodness knows how many years those barns had stood.

Since we children only saw Sunnybank Farm in our school holidays, not many memories could be recalled, except one in particular.

The farm had a big problem, which handicapped all farming aspects. It grew and was swamped by a rogue grass called Johnson grass. This alarming, prolific plant grew so fast, so strong, so tall, that even aboard a moving tractor it was nigh impossible to see where one was going.

A man called Mr Johnson had introduced this grass to Africa – Sunnybank in particular – from where? We could only think from hell! There was no controlling this grass, and the more it was mowed under the more it sprang up, stronger than ever.

Mum sat many days with one of us children on the tractor trying to see where one was going and trying to mow the grass down to clear the lands for planting, with not much luck. After each exhausting day, a sandwich and tea in the fields for lunch, we would drive back to the house on the tractor, worn out.

Mum started to develop enormous boils on her legs; it was from the seeds of the Johnson grass that had embedded into her legs. Every night she would sit in a chair with her legs in a bucket of hot water, trying to draw the boils to a head. Her legs swelled up alarmingly until she was hardly able to walk, let alone drive a tractor.

Sunnybank was appropriately named; it was really very sunny and hot.

Mum had acquired another dog, this time called Sally, a Rhodesian ridgeback. She was a lovely looking fawn coloured dog, with a ridge running the length of her back.

No one had told Mum that Ridgebacks do not like children. Sally would lie for hours in the blazing sun. Alice, thinking she would get sick or sunstroke at least, tried one day to lift her out of the sun into the shade. Sally leapt up and gave Alice a nasty bite, just above her eye, where she bears the scar to this day.

It seemed to rain only once at Sunnybank Farm, and there was such joy that Dad insisted we all go out naked and do a rain dance! We loved it, except Mum and Dorothy who absolutely refused to strip off. Goodness knows what the natives thought, though a few joined in, but out of modesty or exhibitionism they wore their war attire, which was not quite appropriate. Us naked beings could feel for a long time that precious rainwater falling wonderfully on our parched bodies.

Mum and Dad made some good friends in the Golden Valley mining area. Another farming family, the Holdernesses, had two children about our ages who went to the local Gatooma school, named after the Governor General, 'Sir John Kennedy School'.

They found the same problems that we had with trying to make the farm a productive enterprise, all to no avail, so they decided to go further a-field to find their utopia – much further a-field. Northern Rhodesia was their destination; unchartered wilderness, just right for the adventurer, the enticement being that after a hundred years the land was yours!

There again, like crown land there was not a single thing on this virgin land; no buildings, no fencing, no borehole; nothing. To make matters worse it was hundreds of miles from anywhere. Mr Holderness was stone deaf, and Mum often worried about them after they left for the sticks.

A year later Mum and Dad went up to see them and were devastated to find how isolated they were. After days of travelling, Mum and Dad eventually found them, and poor Mr Holderness was so glad to see them he threw his hat right up into the air, and Mrs Holderness wept for joy.

They were the first white people they had seen since living there! One wonders if they lived for a hundred years…

Another couple of friends were a Polish family who owned a gold mine. This was the first gold mine we all went down. You had to descend far underground in a bucket and walk along lit passages with running water and frogs jumping about. It was all very interesting and exciting, and the foreman at the top gave us children a lump of rock each that we think had gold in!

The Polish lady used to tell us stories about the last World War in Europe and how when they were lined up to be shot they fell down quickly and pretended to be dead.

She also grew the most amazing roses; her favourite was a black rose, so very dark red that it appeared to be pitch black! She said it was her 'War Rose', bought over from Poland.

We children found Mrs Padevewski fascinating. She had a lot of beautiful china and trinkets in her house (we never had beautiful things like that at home). Mum said it was very European and homely, and we loved looking through them.

Sadly, though, Sunnybank Farm was a disaster. There was never any sign of the sleeping partner, Mr Harnden; he must have been sleeping well away! Dad refused to put any more effect into the project and before the year was out we were off to pastures new.

More farms in better areas!

Yale and Oxford Farms

Wendy, Mum, Dad holding Sandra Jane,
Rodney, Alice Elsie, Dorothy Marlene

Yale and Oxford farms were situated on the Old Chakari Road, about eight miles from Gatooma, a country town on the main line through Southern Rhodesia. Chakari was a great farming area, the soil was red and fertile; excellent for tobacco, maize and cotton.

Dad bought these two farms under the Crown Land System, which meant the land was pure virgin; nothing had been grown on the land before, no fencing or buildings had been built. This was just up Pater's street, a real pioneer project. Certain projects had to be undertaken and completed before the farms were yours. Fencing the many miles in was the first and largest project, which took a big slice of the farming capital.

When we took our train to and from boarding school, we would look out of the carriage window and realise we were looking at our farm boundary, miles and miles of it.

A lot of it was wild country, savannah grasslands filled with wild game like kudu, cheetahs, leopards, monkeys and guinea fowl, amongst others.

It was a lovely area, but with all the hard work of establishing the enterprise, one didn't seem to have the time to fully appreciate the beauty of it all.

Since there was nothing at all on the farm, at the same time as the fencing was taking place a home had to be built; a borehole had to be sunk for water. So a round African *kia* was put up in next to no time – two, in fact – until we made the bricks for our proper home.

A very large double bed was put in one *kia* for us smaller children; goodness knows how it fitted through the narrow door, but it did.

The *kia* was made of poles in a round circle, tied at the top like a wigwam and packed with straw and wet mud. This was most effective, and no rain seemed to get in when it rained in the rainy season, and it remained lovely and cool throughout the long summer. Of course, Southern

Rhodesia never got that terribly hot, even though October was called suicide month.

We used to lie in bed at night and count the spiders at the top of the roof, and watch the lizards running in and out of the cracks. It seems strange that snakes did not join us in bed, as we sighted them almost daily and they loved the warmth.

The violent lightning and thunder did not seem to bother the *kia* structure either, and we used to love lying in bed listening to the great bolts of thunder and watching the flashes of lightning, when the whole place lit up like daylight. We found it very exciting, and strangely never thought of being struck ourselves, even though the natives in the compound a mile away had been set on fire by lightning.

Since we were only home for the school holidays, it was all an adventure for us three younger children; but Dorothy Marlene, being that much older and growing up fast, was highly embarrassed that we were living like the natives.

Dad loved it and Mum as usual made the best of everything, even cooking on a wood stove under the trees. It was quite practical, as you knew it would not rain out of season, which was nine months of the year.

At weekends Dad would be up at the crack of dawn with his rifle to go and get us some bacon, literally! One Sunday morning Mum was cooking us a large egg, bacon and sausage breakfast when there was a great rustling and flurry in the undergrowth and a huge wild warthog flew past, knocking Mum over and the frying pan with her! Dad was not far behind, and with a single shot secured our breakfasts for the next few weeks, lovely pork chops as well.

We cannot remember where we bathed, as there was no river on Yale Farm, but we all remember Dad sinking the borehole. He would sit for hours on top of the large anthill, studying the instruction book on how to sink a borehole. He was one of those people who had to do everything himself. Alice would study the book with him and was quite intrigued by the pictures of long narrow tubes with an inner tube.

It was wonderful when at last it was sunk and water just pumped out at the touch of a lever. No excuse for not bathing now!

The loo was one of the first huts built of straw and mud and became a permanent fixture. It was quite peaceful on its own, surrounded by bush, and was always warm inside, with lizards, spiders and the odd snake to keep one company. It was a sheer drop down for the refuse, and we never did know what happened thereafter. Probably the bush looks after itself!

There was a collection of Rhode Island red hens and white Leghorns who were allowed to roam all over the bush; it was only with loud clacking that you knew an egg had been laid, then the hunt was on to find the nest.

Now and again chicks were hatched from a hidden nest and it was sweet to see them following their mother hen around. We did not like it when Dad twisted a hen's neck for the odd dinner, but it was not often, as we never seemed to be short of meat or the inevitable mealies.

There was one hen, called Hetty, who always insisted on laying her daily egg on the floor in the corner of the loo, a lovely brown egg which mum always gave to Rodney for his breakfast, as Hetty was his hen.

The grass grew thick and fawn coloured around the loo and the wooden stove, and sometimes you could not see the stove until you nearly fell over it, if the grass had not been cut for a while.

Mum's weekly letters to us at boarding school, were all about getting the grass cut for our holidays and how many snakes her and the 'house boy', Chibwa, had killed that week. We knew that Mum never killed a snake, because as she said, 'Everything has a reason for being', and as long as the snakes did not come into the house, she let them be.

Juma and common boomslang (tree snake)

Once Dad had the virgin land stumped of all trees and made arable, acres and acres of maize were planted. This, of course, was the staple diet of Africa, and became ours as well. We always knew what we were going to have for lunch in the school holidays; boiled mealies, again and again!

On our second school holidays (there were three holidays a year) Dad had decided the time had come to build our house; but first we had to make the bricks.

We three younger children loved this, as we stood in big potholes up to our armpits with pools of mud in front of us. The idea was to mix the mud up to the right consistency and lever it into the moulds, which were left to harden, then they were stacked into a kiln and fired. This went on all the holidays and we don't know how many hundreds of bricks we made, but it was enough to build our house.

Dorothy refused to get into the potholes; so her job was tractor driving, ploughing and cleaning rows and rows of small maize of weeds. Once the tractor driver had left for home at four thirty, Dorothy's job would begin, and for the next three hours until it got dark at about seven.

Now we think about it, it must have been like slave labour; but it was a good, clean, open life, and we all felt like we were building up our home from scratch, which we were.

When we arrived back for the next school holidays, the house had already been built, with a big veranda or porch on the one side, where we younger children slept in a line, with mosquito nets hung above the beds.

There seemed to be a bit of a problem with the chimney, (goodness knows why one was needed as it never got below fifteen degrees centigrade), so it was knocked down and rebuilt three times; Dad had to get it right.

Mum called it (the house) 'The house, that Jack built'. When we went back years later to Yale Farm only the chimney was standing!

The porch of the house had a long, open window, with no protection from the elements. In the rainy season the rain poured in and we nearly got drowned in our beds! Luckily we thought it was great fun, as Mum used to creep about putting raincoats on our beds for some protection.

It was always amazing that we never all got malaria, as mosquitoes were rife in the rainy season and the constant drone they made was a natural part of bedside life. Mum unfortunately *did* contract malaria, which reoccurred every year at the same time; she was violently ill. She would vomit yellow bile continually, shiver and shake and ran very high temperatures. This would continue for about three weeks, and she would end up looking yellow and very weak. Dad said he thought it would kill her in the end; thank goodness it never did!

Mum in the maize

Farm and Other Animals

Mum had decided to start a dairy farm. Coming from a very big dairy farm in Tockholes, Lancashire, Mum loved all things big (maybe that's why she married Dad!). Seeing that her favourite animal was an elephant and not a viable option, dairy cows it was.

The cows were mainly Frieslands with a few Jerseys, for their cream. Being Mum, all the cows had names and knew exactly which stall to go into to be milked. They had their names on plaques above each stall. We three younger children swore they could read!

So it was that twice a day each cow made its own way up to the dairy to be milked. The produce in the trough must have been very enticing as they came up of their own accord. The milk then had to be taken into Gatooma, the main town, each day.

When Dorothy started work at Barclays Bank as a teller, it was her job, or one of them, to collect and deliver for the farm.

We often had the feeling that the milk cheque was our bread and butter money, as everything else took so long to come in. Never mind, we now had a staple diet of eggs, milk, mealies and meat to live off, all home grown. So it wasn't too bad, after all.

Mum was still spoiling her cows and had a remedy for making a sick cow well; she fed it African beer, from a long bottle tipped down its throat. They seemed to get wise to this treatment, and one Friesland cow in particular called Daisy became a real alcoholic and would moo very loudly and even come up to the house making a terrific noise and try to get into the kitchen. Mum insisted she was in pain and would go down to the compound a mile away and get from the natives a bucket or two of raw African beer.

You could actually see Daisy smacking her lips in glee.

Dad would get very cross and slap Daisy on the behind and say, 'Off with you!' She would moo even louder, dribbling beer out of the corners of her mouth. Mum insisted that Daisy was the best milker, and boy what milk!

There would be long and heated arguments between our parents over the 'cost of production' at the dairy. We felt, though, that it stopped Mum being homesick for England.

Dad also had his 'soft spot'; he loved all small beings – babies, animals; anything. There was a funny little chicken, the runt of the litter so to speak, called Chicory, who would insist on sitting on Dad's knee when he sat down, or on his shoulder when he was walking about.

No one else was allowed to touch him; he would chirp loudly and peck any other person who came remotely near. Chicory was most strange looking and we often wondered if indeed he was a chicken at all…

Dad never believed in idleness, and the few times we managed to get into Gatooma it was not to the picture house or 'bioscope' as it was called in Rhodesia (by the Afrikaans speaking people). We loved both, so a good cooling down swim and a couple of good books was the answer to a few hours away from the farm.

Dad had a habit, which we all followed, of reading at the dining table. Only Mum, doing all the work of serving up and clearing away (with the houseboy, Chibwa), did not read a book. We thought this was quite normal, and even today we can all do two or three things together with complete concentration.

Alice asked Dad to bring her a library book back one morning when dropping the milk in town. He bought back *Molly has a Quiet Time*, which upset Alice terribly, so the next time he bought her *Beyond the Black Stump* by Neville Shute, and Alice was hooked and read all his books. Dad then bought her from the library *Of Human Bondage*, by Somerset Maugham, and so started a love affair with the greatest writer that ever lived, according to Alice.

Alice (and probably her siblings) in sheer peace, in the loo outside, read *Lady Chatterley's Lover*, which just happened to be on the house bookshelf. 'Oh for a Woodcutter!'

Long hours of peace would descend over the house in the evenings, as everybody just read and read.

We always said Dad's saving grace was his sense of humour, which could only have been English. Sometimes the meal times would go on and on, with dad holding forth with his tales and jokes. Rodney was often the brunt of these jokes, as he was very good-looking and Dad insisted he should be a rock star, which Rodney hated. We would all join in with the ribbing, and it became quite a rabble.

In hindsight, Dad was quite right; what with Rodney's looks and a bit of musical training, we felt sure he would have surpassed the future Elvis. Who knows?

Wendy, being frail and whimsical, was also the academic of the family, with a heart of gold, like Mum. No suffering missed her attention, and she was always the first to reach out. The Piccanins loved her, and she was always ready with a paper and pencil to teach them how to write their names. When at Queen Elizabeth High School, Wendy obtained high results in the Cambridge leaving exams and turned into a rare classical beauty.

Alice always used to tell the tale of people asking her, 'Are there more like you at home?' They were stunned and bowled over when meeting Wendy!

We often wondered what Arnold would have been like if he had lived, as he was the image of Dad, and it was obvious Dad would never get over the loss of his oldest son.

Being virgin land and new to development, Yale and Oxford farms were still populated by all creatures great and small. The snakes quickly adapted to us humans sharing their space – well, they were there first, as Mum said – and took full advantage of all we had to offer.

Mum noticed that the brown egg that Hetty laid daily in the warmth of the loo hut was trailing off, and soon found out the reason why. One morning there was a very loud, aggressive clucking from Hetty and Mum, hurrying to the loo, was just in time to see a huge boomslang – a tree snake – with an egg in its mouth, sliding away. Poor

Hetty was perched on top of the loo, clucking loudly.

Needless to say, Mum just chased the snake away with a big stick and carried indignant Hetty inside for a special treat.

Snakes love warmth, and as it was nearly always hot outside, it was not unusual to see them curled up asleep on the tractors seats.

There were two tractors on Yale Farm; a big John Deere and a smaller Massey Ferguson. Dorothy drove both in her duties as a tractor driver, but we younger siblings only drove the Massey Ferguson short distances, like to the dairy and back.

Alice, one morning on going to move the tractor to the dairy, had the fright of her life. She didn't find the usual snake on the seat; but on holding the tractor steering wheel she had both hands on a small, entwined snake wrapped around the steering wheel in a neat, complete circle! Who got the biggest shock was debateable; the snake, still dazed from its slumber, just fell onto Alice's lap, then dropped gracefully to the ground and slid just as slowly away.

Looking back, it was amazing no one got bitten; but as we had all taken on board that we shared this wonderful environment with all God's creatures, it became just part of everyday life.

Virginia Tobacco – The Cash Crop

Pater – in the tobacco field

After the house Dad built the tobacco barns; we are not convinced they were built with our homemade bricks, as they are still standing today, unlike our house.

Growing Virginia tobacco, curing it, grading it and baling it, was a long, labour intensive procedure. It was a matter of 'all hands on deck' from the start. That included Piccanins and us children; in fact all able beings.

The tobacco plant is related to such plants as the tomato and potato. It first grew in Caribbean countries and in Mexico and South America. Cultivated tobacco is an annual plant and grows to approximately four to six feet. Producing about twenty and sometimes thirty leaves, it measures from twenty-four to thirty inches long and fifteen to eighteen inches wide. The tobacco plant ranges from light green to dark green in colour. A vigorous, mature plant produces a million seeds yearly – enough to plant about one hundred acres of tobacco.

The procedure starts with the planting of seedbeds in early spring, which are covered with cloth or plastic. The plants grow six to eight inches in eight to twelve weeks, and then are transplanted out into the ready ploughed fields. This planting season always coincided with our Christmas holidays and the rain. As soon as the seedlings reached their appropriate height, all hands were needed to transplant into the fields.

An adult native would walk in front with a *badga*, make a slot in the already turned earth and small hands (usually one of us children or a Piccanin), would deposit a little healthy tobacco seedling neatly into the hole, cover over with the rich, loose soil, and press firmly down with feet.

This went on up and down long rows, usually in driving rain (which was the ideal planting weather), from the early hours of the morning, usually four o'clock. Mum would come out of the farmhouse at about eight with huge pans of mealie meal porridge and big urns of sweet tea for all us workers.

It was really rewarding to see those little plants standing proudly in long rows, up and down acres and acres of fields. We always found it remarkable that every plant survived; there were no blank patches in the fields, absolutely none!

It rained solidly for three months and the little tobacco plants grew and grew, taller and taller.

The soil between the rows of tobacco would be cultivated to keep it loose and to remove any weeds that sprang up.

Once the plant reaches twenty-four inches in height, the upper part is 'topped' off when the plant begins to produce flowers; this makes the leaves grow larger and heavier.

The tobacco plants grow in the fields in the rainy season for about three months, and one prays that there are no hailstorms to damage the leaves and that the leaves are the right colour and texture: not too dark in colour, therefore being difficult to cure; or too light weight, therefore crumbling at touch after curing. In other words, just right!

There was, all in all, a fine art in getting the right leaf.

After three months of growing in the fields, and when the rain stops, the tobacco leaves are ripe for picking.

One starts picking from the ground up, as the biggest leaves are always at the bottom. These leaves are then stacked onto a trailer, driven by a tractor and taken to the big, high barns for stacking and curing. The leaves are twisted in pairs onto poles, and starting from the top of the barns, laid in layers all the way down to the bottom.

Once a barn is full a temperature gauge is set and a furnace (heated by wood fires outside) heats the air, which fans through the drying leaves. This is called 'flue cured' and is mainly used for the making of cigarettes. This usually takes about a week for each full barn, and the temperature and moisture context have to be checked regularly so the leaves don't become too dry and brittle.

Once the leaves are cured, then the poles are removed, the leaves untied and laid in heaps on the grading shed floor, ready for 'grading'. Again all hands were needed, and wives usually came forward with all their family, even breast-feeding babies, as the days were long and busy.

The leaves are put into different piles; first, second and third. This is the grading procedure, and it all depends on the colour, texture, weight and lack of blemishes, the first grade being golden in colour, heavy weight with absolutely no blemishes; and so on.

Pater – in Virginia tobacco

The grading shed was a hub of activity, with women, children and babies taking part in the grading of the golden leaves and putting them in neat piles. Mum would arrive at about midday with urns of tea and big trays of sticky buns (these were bought daily from Gatooma, after the milk was delivered). They (the buns) were beautiful and fresh with currants and topped with icing sugar, a great favourite with the Piccanins.

There were the overseers, qualified males who regularly checked the bundles. Once a bundle became large enough and certified as to the quality for that grade, it was put into a large press and then pressed down very tight to create a big square bundle of cured tobacco, covered by strong brown wrapping paper on all sides.

The tobacco dust in the grading shed was quite thick, and the sun shining in through open doors and windows would make beautiful shapes and patterns, and the golden tobacco leaves looked more golden then ever, filling one's nose with strong perfumes of indescribable smells. The small children would sneeze and cough continually, and had to be removed quite often at intervals to clear their throats and heads.

Mum and Wendy could not take much of the strong tobacco smell, but Rodney and Alice loved it and never coughed.

Once the bales were filled and pressed down to create neat tight parcels, there was then the problem of where to store them, in a dry, safe area, before they were taken in bulk to the tobacco auctions in Salisbury.

As Dad had not yet built a shed it was decided to store the bales in the lounge of the farmhouse, much to Mum and Dorothy's horror!

They were stacked high to the rafters of the house (there was not yet a ceiling – no money yet). We three younger children had a great time climbing up and down the bales. Poor Dorothy was mortified. Being a very good looking girl, she had a few really nice admirers and was so embarrassed when they knocked on the front door to take her out for the evening to be met by huge bales of tobacco instead of a nice sitting area. The trials and tribulations of being the eldest were many, and sometimes too much for poor Dorothy to bear.

One of the hardest and most critical parts of the tobacco process was keeping the barn fires lit, and at the right temperature, throughout the curing stage.

The furnaces were at the back of the barns and had to be manned day and night. The problems always occurred at night; a native would be on duty but would invariable fall asleep from midnight onwards unless checked.

Dad, by this time having got both Oxford and Yale fully productive with maize, tobacco, dairy and beef, was onto other enterprises; a ranch filled with Afrikaner beef cattle, and even further a-field in

Malawi helping President Banda with his huge tobacco schemes.

So the running of Yale and Oxford was mostly left to Mum, which meant during the period the tobacco curing was taking place she would get out of bed two or three times from midnight onwards to check on the barn furnaces and to see that the native on duty was awake; which he never was!

The producing of Virginia tobacco as a cash crop was all very hard work, involving a lot of people, but it was worth it in the end, because once the bales were sent to the auctions, money just rolled in. Thank goodness!

Yale and Oxford farms were rewarding enterprises, and even though a lot of work had to be done at the onset – like stumping the virgin land of all trees and roots, then ploughing and cultivating – the results were great as the soil was of high standard; deep red, with plenty of top soil undamaged.

It was full-time, very time consuming, and we often wondered why none of us ever smoked and hated mealies for lunch!

Farm Assistants

With Dad being a teacher of agriculture rather than a 'long-term farmer', he obviously felt his side of the job was complete once he had got things up and running.

In the case of Sunnybank Farm, being an old established concern, the hard work such as tree stumping, fencing, buildings and so on had already been done. Even so, the up-keep of this difficult farm was horrendous and Dad decided to get Mum some help before he left to start other businesses.

So, Dad employed a farm assistant for Mum, and like his successor he was an alien from another country. Dad got his assistants from advertisements in the *Farmers' Weekly*, which stated 'highly qualified young man'. These young men had never been to, let alone seen Africa in their lives!

Mum was horrified, but as Dad quickly disappeared, she decided to give it a go, and set the young farm assistant his tasks.

The farm assistant at Sunnybank Farm was from Switzerland; a very fair skinned, blond haired man called Hans, extremely nervous of the sun, snakes and Friday night 'tonk-ups' in the compound by the natives.

Mum started him on the far side of the farm, clearing the land of Johnson grass, ploughing the fields, cultivating and planting the maize seeds. Hans, poor chap, would return at night on the tractor burnt bright red, no matter how much sun cream Mum insisted on covering him with.

Coming from a 'precise', well organised country like Switzerland, Hans just could not understand the native culture and that just about no one came to work on Monday after a weekend of heavy revelling! It was impossible to expect anywhere near half attendance.

Hans kept strict records of who came to work, at what time and what their job was. Since he made up the weekly wage packet, it was near murder on Friday evenings when the natives discovered their pay had been docked for non-attendance on Monday.

To save us from a crisis, Mum had a quick word with the supervisor in Shona (which she had quickly mastered); the natives then accepted their short paid wages meekly, and then were given the extra day's pay by the supervisor. With this system in operation, murder was averted and Hans' pride not dented.

Hans seemed to master his fear of snakes – and there were plenty – but his nights were wracked with nightmares. As there was no separate cottage, Hans had the spare bedroom in the house, and you could tell he was thankful to be under the family roof. The big spiders that came out at night to eat the mosquitoes added to his nightmares, and he sometimes never stopped trembling.

Mum told him again and again that nature had a system; the mosquitoes 'ate' us so the spiders ate the mosquitoes! She never told him about the dry land scorpions whose bite could be fatal and the pain unbearable. Luckily, there was never one hiding in his boots, even though we children showed him how to turn his boots upside down before putting them on in the mornings.

What really sent poor Hans packing for home was not snakes, scorpions or natives but the elements; nature itself.

The rainy season could be violent, really violent, and even though Sunnybank Farm never seemed to get much rain, it had the most horrific 'dry storms'. Thunder and lightning would go on for hours, as if the end of the world was upon us. It was extremely dangerous, and many a native *kia* was struck and set on fire by the lightning, the people inside struck dead, sometimes turned to *chaco*.

It used to start with the thunder, a loud rumble and then a loud crack, and suddenly the heavens lit up with flashes of lightning. It was unbelievable and unknown anywhere but in the tropics.

We children all thought it was wonderful, though the dogs used to howl and go crazy, running round and round. But poor Hans was the worst affected; he became demented. He screamed, hid under the bed and as a last resort rushed to Mum's room and got into bed with her! Luckily Dad was not there (Mum was herself only a few years older than Hans). Mum would cover up his head and rock the sobbing young man backwards and forwards until the storm was over, which could be ages. We were all mystified as to Hans' reaction, even though we realised it was really terrifying, as there was all that noise, lightning, but no rain!

Dorothy would make us all tea, which definitely helped.

Hans never did get used to the force of nature; he said it was evil forces! And who would argue?

Before the rainy season was out, Hans had decided to call it a day and left on the next ship to Switzerland. Bless him!

Farm assistants at Yale and Oxford farms were a necessity as both farms were fully productive and it was impossible for just Mum to oversee them.

The first two assistants were much of a haze, completely unsuitable even though they came from the same *Farmers' Weekly* resort, with the same good recommendation of being 'highly qualified young men'.

The first young farm assistant we recalled at Yale/Oxford was with us for a very short time. Completely foreign in every way, his name was unpronounceable, also we were not sure what language he spoke, but he kept saying 'OK' to everything, so we decided to call him 'OK'!

OK resided in one of the nearby *kias* and settled in quite happily. In no time at all he had gathered vegetables from the kitchen garden and cooked himself a wonderful vegetable stew.

He was a very rotund, pleasant fellow, always smiling.

Mum took him over to Oxford Farm, which was quite far away from Yale, and left him with a gang of natives stacking the maize and removing the mealies to be sent to Yale Farm to be milled into mealie meal.

Mum had to keep going over to check on how OK was managing, as the native supervisor, Isaac, was worried about him, as he said he just sat under a tree all day eating and drinking!

OK would take a big hamper with him daily, but it was not a good example for the working natives. Mum said he was depressed and very lonely for his own kind, which was a problem for us all.

We children only saw him the one holiday, and we never did know what language he spoke or what country he came from; but we all wished OK well.

When we came home for the Christmas holidays there was another farm assistant installed and living in the farm *kia*.

This young man was called Tich, for the reason that he was ever so tall and exceptionally thin. Tich seemed to fit in quite well and spoke English with a heavy German accent and smoked non-stop.

Dad had introduced the Afrikaner cattle to Yale Farm, for their beef, so Tich would go off for the whole day to the far end of Yale Farm, checking the cattle and the fences.

There was a lot to be done with all the cattle, both beef and dairy, such as dipping, branding, de-horning, castrating and so on.

Mum was very worried when Tich decided to 'ride the cattle' through the dip, which was an arsenic mixture. Strangely, it did not seem to affect him!

When we returned for the next school holidays Tich was no longer with us. Apparently, as most of our neighbours were German, Tich had formed other friendships and moved on.

There was a lull for a while with no farm assistant, just Mum and her supervisor, Isaac, who was actually very efficient. The workload, though, became too much. Mum had decided to try and recoup some of the weekly wages she and other farms paid out; so she decided to open a store on the corner where four farms joined. There was no other retail outlet for miles, so it did excellent business. Yale Store became very popular and catered for all the natives' needs, such as groceries, sticky buns, paraffin, matches and even plenty of colourful cloths for homemade dresses and shirts.

Mum used to make us laugh when she told the tale of how the native wives had to have exactly the same amount of cloth, no matter what size they were; remember most natives had more than one or two wives, out of necessity.

The shop was also a meeting place, and many friendships were formed on the shop step. It was a source of holiday pocket money for us children, as the shop had to be manned at all times.

Then Mum got another and the strangest of all farm assistants (if that was possible); Azez, who was a stunningly good-looking Egyptian, with the same credentials as the others: 'highly qualified young man'. Azez was tall, slim, with a lock of jet black hair which flopped attractively over one eye. Azez had two obsessions: one, Dorothy Marlene; and two, laboratory experiments.

Both seemed to go together, for as soon as Azez knew Dorothy was in the vicinity he would open his trunk of test tubes,

Bunsen burners, coloured and uncoloured bottles, and conduct some form of experiment on the lounge floor. No one was impressed except we three younger children, as we were always interested in what went in one end and came out the other.

It was a painstaking job, making distilled water for the tractors and truck batteries. It just dripped out so slowly, and didn't look any different from when it went in! Mum kept telling Azez that rainwater would do just as well, but as Azez pointed out, it only rained three months of the year; quite right too!

Dorothy Marlene was so unimpressed that she could not wait for Mum to 'sign him off', and was furious with Dad for being continually away, now with President Banda in Malawi and his tobacco schemes.

Dorothy Marlene, David Robinson, Wendy, Alice, Rodney

Little Golden Haired Girl

Sandra Jane Bell – Shaney – Pippin – Wiggy

The whole household knew something was a foot for quite a few months, as there were a lot of mutterings from Dorothy: 'Disgusting, they should know better and should be ashamed of themselves, especially at their age!'

These remarks were directed at Mum and Dad, and were received with black looks from Dad and furtive looks from Mum. Bearing in mind Mum was at the time thirty-seven and Dad forty-three, maybe they were not so old to bear another child!

We younger children knew it was something 'bad', but as life was full of holidays and boarding school, we didn't have much time to dwell on the dark forecasts. Until one school holiday, that is, when on arriving home, Mum said, 'Come and look here, but under no circumstances wake her up!' There, on the porch, lying in a pram with a green mosquito net over the top, was a tiny golden haired little girl, who opened her dark brown eyes and looked at us all leaning over the pram. She let out an enormous scream and Mum came running over, lifted her high sky and laid Sandra Jane in our waiting arms.

Sandra Jane, who called herself Shaney and was named Pippin (a rosy English apple) by Dad, Wiggy by Dorothy and her lovely boyfriend David, and Spoilt Brat by Alice, Wendy and Rodney, was completely spoilt from birth.

The local doctor refused to deliver a baby on April Fools Day, so Shaney had to wait to make her appearance on the 2nd April 1954. Dorothy immediately took Shaney under her wing, gave her a bottle before she went to work in Gatooma and took her from Mum when she arrived back in the evenings.

Mum, of course, was still up to her eyes in work on the farm, so with Dad coming and going, we children – especially Dorothy – were a great help.

Dad was over the moon with his Pippin, the apple of his eye! She seemed at last to fill that void that Arnold's death had left.

Shaney was a born manipulator – she called it 'organiser' later in life – and was completely the centre of all attention and spoilt rotten, but loved very dearly!

When we came home on school holidays, Shaney took full advantage of her big sisters and adoring brother.

Shaney had followed Mum's example and became very fond of the dairy cows. She became so fond that she developed a strange desire/demand to have her meals sitting on a cow's back! But not just any cow – no, not Daisy the alcoholic, but another Friesland called Rosie.

Rosie really took a liking to Shaney and would lick her legs with her rough tongue. Shaney said it was kisses, but Mum said Rosie liked the salt. Rosie would stand quite still whilst Shaney ate her meal, looking quite triumphantly at us below on the ground. A right little minx our Shaney was!

So now there was Rosie coming up to the gate, mooing loudly, every afternoon at about five o'clock, this time not for beer, like Daisy, but for Shaney to come running out with her plate of food, and of course something for Rosie, who was partial to apples and carrots.

Who says animals aren't intelligent?

How that little blond haired girl got her own way again and again takes the cake.

Shaney also became a favourite with the natives on the farm, and was called Piccaniny Goose Gas. In fact, her first normal meal was eaten in a native *kia*, and consisted of mealy meal, pumpkin and rape (like open leaf cabbage). In fact Shaney was the first in the family to 'go native' and eat what the indigenous ate.

To this day, Mum, Dad and Dorothy never eat pumpkin and rice as a vegetable, only as a pudding – rice pudding and pumpkin fritters, which are delicious.

Shaney was hyperactive and in no time was playing cricket with Rodney and us sisters, where she became a first-class runner. At school later on she became known as Springkaan, a slim quick deer of delightful colouring.

From a very early age, Shaney seemed 'at one' with all the farm animals, especially the dogs, which there was an assortment of. With her being so much younger than the rest of her siblings, Shaney often appeared to be an only child, so her company then was her four-legged friends.

One of Shaney's stunts was to put the kitchen chairs in a circle and get each dog to sit on them, then stand on their back legs, on command! It was quite a feat for a tiny girl to do, and amazingly the dogs obeyed her. She was a strong natured little soul, in more ways than one!

Shaney, of course, was the only Rhodesian 'born and bred' in the family, and looked quite different from us all, with her blond hair and brown, naughty eyes.

She was probably the nearest to Dad in looks – he had deep brown eyes, and they could both look at you with sharp intensity.

Also they both had that fantastic sense of humour which could only be British.

Dad and Shaney were 'one of a pair'.

Dad had at last found his soul mate in the form of a little blond haired girl.

Mum, Shaney, Sally and Ben

Locusts, Armyworms and Field Mice

Some alarming disasters disrupted farming in Africa on a national scale. Swarms of locusts descending on an area were a frightening sight. Normally farmers were alerted to these outbreaks, but the first sighting at Yale Farm was totally unexpected.

One mid-spring afternoon we were all outside near the dairy when a dark cloud descended over us all. It was very difficult to make out what was happening, when all of a sudden funny looking green grasshoppers dropped out of the sky in vast numbers, completely covering the area.

It was an alarming sight, as it took some time to realise what on earth was happening, and whatever these large winged creatures were.

As they dropped to the ground with a heavy plonk, they immediately started to eat everything in sight. The grass disappeared within minutes, and then they swarmed in their tens of millions onto the young maize crop.

It was quite incredible; in no time there was not a young maize plant left standing, as far as the eye could see. We could not believe what we were seeing, this seething mass of green insects buzzing and munching away; you could actually hear them munching! It was like watching a horror film; we could only gape in disbelief.

Then, just as quickly as these 'grasshopper greens' had descended, they up and left, leaving not a green blade of grass or crop in sight!

The UN organisation says a fully fledged locust plague has the potential of damaging the livelihood of a tenth of the world's population; and we can certainly believe that after what we witnessed! It was a sight second to none. We only hoped Dad was insured against these plagues, as it was too late in the season to replant the maize fields. Thank goodness we remember seeing only three of these plagues in all our time at Yale and Oxford farms.

Locusts were not the only disaster to befall us; the dreaded armyworm affected all our lives on the farm, far worse and for a much longer time then the locust plague.

The armyworm, or caterpillar, is usually the larvae of the moth spodoptera frugiperda. Female moths lay egg masses on leaf blades. The caterpillars vary tremendously in colour, from light green to brown to almost black. They have three yellow stripes on the back which join at the head. Larvae feed on the leaves and stems of any young plant and usually pupate in the soil or leaf sheath. They can suddenly appear in huge numbers to ravage land and crops.

Records describe armies of caterpillars swarming over hundreds of square miles; they can contain so many insects that trains can't grip the tracks and cars slide off the road. The insects, true to their name, form veritable armies, up to one thousand one hundred per square metre. Crops, pasture, school fields, even village football pitches were under attack. Small children refused to leave their homes for the fear of this crawling invasion.

The armyworm has become more of a threat in recent years. This is due to an increase in population, the intensified use of rangeland for feeding livestock and possibly global warming.

So with all this devastating knowledge, it was with very heavy hearts that we would receive a letter from Mum at boarding school to tell us that the armyworms were back! They were right, at that time, in full force, destroying all the maize fields on both Oxford and Yale Farms.

We children would have little or no wish to go home for the school holidays, because it just meant work and more work for us. At the break of the day we would be issued with bottles of warm soapy water and sent in a long line up and down the rows of maize, shaking the mixture from the bottle down the sheaf of the maize. Caterpillars used to fall to the ground in their hundreds, but it was uncertain whether they were dead, as they were still wiggling about. It was an exhausting and soulless way to spend one's precious holidays, as the end of the epidemic was never in sight.

Mum would not allow us to go to Oxford Farm, where the worms were, if it were at all possible, more dense; in fact the fields of maize just looked like a mass of black waves! The whole season's harvest was a write off, and Dad's morale would reach an all-time low.

It was devastating.

Thank goodness that in all the years at Yale and Oxford farms the armyworm plague only struck us twice (it seemed to surface every seven years), but that was certainly enough for anyone!

The scourge of the field mice (if you can call it that) was the least threatening and certainly not devastating like the other two epidemics.

Once the maize was harvested and stacked in the fields, the field mice appeared in droves from under the soil. It was a signal for everybody to get into action. Rodney would be out day after day with his air gun, popping them off; the dogs would go crazy, flying around chasing them, and the natives would collect as many dead ones as possible for their cooking pots!

It was pandemonium for a few days on each field. Poor little mice didn't stand a chance.

Run Little Field Mouse, Run!

Fat ones, thin ones
Black ones, white ones
Happy ones, sad ones
Cheeky ones, sleepy ones
Bewildered ones, cross ones
They all ran for their lives
To another happy hunting ground
Down under.

Our Extended Black Family

We were lucky with our native employees; it was just like a big happy family. Farm life was so busy all the year round that the whole family were employed some of the time in the grading shed, and at other times busy on the lands planting tobacco seedlings.

A few of the natives, like Chibwa, who worked in the house, and Juma, the gardener, came with us from Sunnybank Farm in Golden Valley.

The natives would live in what was commonly known as a compound of *kias* grouped together. The *kias* on Yale Farm were not brick-built like on Little England Estates, but like the more common type; made from sticks and mud. Water was obtained from a couple of communal taps, and the fires for cooking were usually made outside. The staple diet was mealie meal and a green vegetable, which looked like an open cabbage, called rape. The mealie meal was not eaten as the white people eat it (as a porridge), but as a firm lump called *sudza*. The *sudza* would be rolled into a hard ball by the hands and dipped into a meat stew. It was actually delicious, and was Shaney's first real meal!

Sometimes the maize was eaten as 'corn on the cob', not boiled but roasted over the fire on a grid. You liked it or you didn't; we children found the mealies cooked this way too hard to eat. Mum would always boil the mealie for ten minutes and then cover with farm butter. Yummy, if you did not have to have it every day; which we usually did!

Of course Friday was the beer brewing day, all day, and this was undertaken by the *umdelas* – older women of the farm – and made in a huge empty petrol drum. It was left festering over a fire all day, where it would bubble away, and certain strange things were thrown in!

Now and again a wooden spoon would be pushed into our mouths, but it tasted so bitter and vile that only Shaney seemed to lick her lips and ask for more! Rodney thought it was horrible, as he also said he saw them – the women – throw mice into the drum, claws and all; very possible, as nothing on the farm was wasted.

There was also a lot of smoking going on amongst the natives, and even though some bought cigarettes from the store, most rolled their own from the dagga leaf, which grew right there with their own mealies.

As none of our family ever smoked, we never had the pleasure of smoking our own Virginia tobacco or *dagga*, which Dad said was very good and relaxing for the natives! All we knew was that it took a day of rest on Monday to get over the weekend for the staff. So why not? Life was simple and one could only make use of what was on hand.

Mum and Dad were very tolerant and understanding with all the different ways and customs.

If there was a death in one of the native families, the burial would go on for days, then a couple of months later a second burial for the same person's spirit would take place. This would mean a few more days off work, sometimes over a week. Dad said it was quite right, and gave the bereaved as much time off as required.

Mum was at times – usually night times – called out to a birth (if the pregnant women did not have time to go 'home'). Consequently, there were a few little black girls called Eva, after Mum, who thought the name quite suited them. We girls were encouraged to make baby clothes for them. As we were not a knitting family (except for Dorothy who was too busy), the little girls usually had their dresses made from the bright materials purchased from the store, out of our pocket money.

The little black babies were really cute, with big brown eyes, a ready smile and always so plump and content, mother's milk being the best.

Shaney was the first again to copy the native mothers, and was in no time strapping her dolls on her back. It looked so funny when Shaney got one of the mothers to allow her to strap her child on her back for half an hour; the little blond head next to the little black one, a good picture! Mum would only be worried when Shaney tried to feed the babies toffees and other sweets.

Mum's greatest worry with the babies was with gastric enteritis, which a child could contract at the drop of a hat. The child would develop a severe runny tummy, which just would not clear up. This would very quickly develop into dehydration, and if not attended could lead to death. This could be very sad and very sudden. This was the greatest killer of children in Africa at this time, and not only black children; white children were just as vulnerable.

There were some real characters among the natives on the farm, and Mum made some good friends, especially with the women, who she gave lots of help with the up-bringing of the children.

One character in particular was Juma, who was of an unfathomable age but held a soft spot in all our lives. Juma was a romantic. Wild flowers would appear in bunches in the kitchen. Mum would be delighted, especially if they were her favourite the Flame Lily, the emblem of Rhodesia; so exotic and decorative.

What used to worry Mum about Juma was what he would bring her for Christmas and where he got it from. Dad would kill a beef cow for the natives for their Christmas festive; Juma, not to be outdone, would find something from somewhere for Mum. The first Christmas at Yale Farm Juma arrived with a very large live turkey, and a loudly clucking, beautiful cockerel! Mum was immediately suspicious as to where Juma had got them, and she was quite right not to prepare them immediately for Christmas dinner (even though the turkey looked extremely appetising).

Sure enough, Mum's suspicions were quickly realised when after a few days a policeman (one of the few we ever saw), came to the farm, knocked at the kitchen door and accused us of stealing a big turkey and a Rhode Island red cockerel called 'Pet', belonging to our neighbours, the Taylors. Mum appeared to be very shocked, but with Pet standing on the kitchen chair clucking loudly, the game was up!

Mum and Mrs Taylor had many a laugh about that episode and other requirements Juma got as presents for Mum. Mum said he was a very 'giving man', and his heart was in the right place, bless him.

We all laughed one day when Rodney called Mum to the door saying there was a native looking for work, and could we offer him anything? Mum asked Rodney to ask him what work he had done. The answer came back proudly; he was a carpenter like Jesus. Needless to say he got the job!

Dad had his favourites too. One was a little black girl called Topsy – she was really cute, with enormous brown eyes and her hair tied up with red ribbons into corkscrews.

Her mother, Rachel, was one of Dad's best workers and when she came to work (mainly in the grading shed) she always bought Topsy with her. Dad swore she (Topsy) was the best grader, as her little fingers were soon feeling and sorting the leaves into groups. Dad had a supply of lollipops for her to suck, so she became known by the natives as the Lollipop Girl, and her big brown eyes would light up when she saw Dad, and she would love it when he picked her up and threw her into the air, like he used to do with Shaney.

Wendy made Topsy a rag doll with corkscrew plaits to match hers; Topsy was thrilled and immediately called the doll

Windy, the nearest she could say to Wendy! So very sweet.

We think Dad would have adopted her; another soul mate for him.

Dad said that the natives had the nicest of natures, and he was right.

Friends, Neighbours and the Second World War

The Bell clan and the Crowshaws, another Lancashire family, Gatooma, 1954

Yale and Oxford farms were both down the Old Chakari Road, and so were other farms. Rich red soil and a wonderful climate made this a sought after area, so no land remained vacant from the white farmers.

Southern Rhodesia in the Fifties was a hotchpotch of all nationalities escaping Europe after the Second World War. Businesses sprang up in the towns run by Jewish traders, and farms were bought and acquired by Germans and Dutch and English.

Germans, Dutch and Afrikaners owned most of the farms on the Old Chakari Road. The area was very new, virginal and waiting for development.

The main road had gone one step further than a dirt road and was a strip road, this being just two parallel lengths of tarmac running for miles and miles. For two cars to pass each car had to leave one strip free. Sometimes it was a game of chicken; one car only got off at the last possible minute!

The telephone was another great hazard; it was on a party line, which meant that each number had a certain amount of rings before one picked up the receiver. Ours was three shorts and one long.

The one farmer's wife, Mrs Richter, lived for and on the phone; she picked up the phone on everybody else's ring and often joined in the conservation, especially if it was in German. A real nosy parker!

Our nearest neighbours were English farmers, the Tailors, and we had a friendly relationship with them, their children being same age as the three youngest in our family, but going to day school in Gatooma, not boarding school like us.

Then further away it was the Germans – the Richters, Dutch – the Daniels, and Afrikaners – the Oosthizens.

Everything would have been possibly all right, except that Dad was greatly resented with his 'Oxford' accent, and being a farmer's representative and having to attend all the farmer's meetings, feelings ran high against this big good-looking Englishman! Mum really felt the atmosphere and used to plead with Dad not to go to all these meetings. We think she really feared for his life.

Dorothy was another issue. She was an extremely attractive girl with a figure to die for and wonderful rare oval face, which you really only find on a cameo brooch. Coupled with all these attributes she was blessed with a most refined manner; she really had it all. The lads from the surrounding farms needed a lot of courage to come 'courting' – so much courage in fact that they would come in twos and threes to Yale Farm, but to no avail; Dorothy Marlene would not even see them let alone speak to them!

Month after month this would go on, until Mum really felt sorry for the persistent lads, but was discouraged in no uncertain terms by Dorothy. Then revenge would be sought – especially by the three Richter boys. They would root up the farm disk showing the name of Yale and Oxford Farms at the end of the Old Chakari Road and throw it in the mud.

The war was on.

Dorothy, on her to work at Barclays Bank, would stop, get out of the car in her stilettos and struggle to right the heavy plough disk in deep mud, only to find on her return trip that it was lying down again. Dorothy never gave up, either way! So the war went on.

Dorothy had the most wonderful boyfriends, as being so good-looking and elegant she was spoilt for choice. Both Wendy and Alice fell madly in love with them all, especially David who was greatly amused by all the attention he received when Wendy and Alice came home for the holidays; they would dress up in Dorothy's high-heeled shoes and give a hands-on play nearly every time he put in an appearance, poor chap! It was no wonder he was forever taking Dorothy off to the Eastern highlands for weeks at a time when he knew the young sisters were coming on school holidays.

Dorothy was eventually claimed by and married a handsome farmer from far away, introduced by Dad.

The real character of the area was Farmer Webb, a real Stewart Granger look alike, who was well into his seventies and a great favourite with the ladies. Tall, upright, with devastating good looks, he was out to kill, especially when he put on what he called his 'courting boots'. These were leather leggings, well polished, and they shone with success.

Farmer Webb was managing Oxford Farm after Dad had sold it to Pat Conway, the hotelier in Gatooma.

Farmer Webb soon realised mum was the belle of the ball in the area and often on her own with Dad away with his farming scheme commitments.

Most evenings Farmer Webb would don his courting boots and drive over to Yale Farm where Mum would invariably invite him to stay for dinner. Farmer Webb had many tales to tell of his life in South Africa in the early days, friends with the African chiefs. He spoke Korsa fluently, which was delightful to hear, as there was a lot of clicking of the tongue.

He was at one time mauled by a lion and in hospital for a long time, and bitten by a snake, which bite he cut out himself and sucked out the poison. His tales were thrilling for us children and he well earned his supper.

He used to call Mum his 'little sunflower'. Of course she was only in her thirties, but we thought it was her sunny, lovely nature he was referring to, as much as to her good looks.

We all adored Farmer Webb and he was made most welcome at Yale Farm, not realising that little Shaney felt some resentment against his attentions to Mum and was missing her father.

Once, following Dad's reappearance after a long absence of many months, Shaney dropped a bombshell one evening when we were all having supper around the kitchen table. She stated loud and clear, 'Farmer Webb kissed Mum!' There was a stunned silence, you could hear a pin drop and time was frozen.

Then all of a sudden Dad reached across the table and slapped Mum hard across the face, knocking her clean off the chair.

Mum got up off the kitchen floor and left the room; we did not see her until the next morning.

Wendy and Alice gave Shaney a good hitting, but she protested in her clear, piping voice that it was true, Farmer Webb *did* kiss Mum, and she saw! But why be a tell-tale, we asked?

Funnily, Farmer Webb arrived the next afternoon with his arm full of wild flowers from Oxford for us all. Dad fixed him with a steely look, and in no time at all everything was back to normal.

Needless to say Dad did not leave on another sojourn for a few months.

Alice had an admirer on her school holidays, the son of the local cinema owner in town. The cinema was affectionately called the 'fleapit'; lots of scratching – amongst other things – went on, but as the films were free, Alice said it was a welcome relief from the hard work of farming!

Wendy, Dorothy Marlene, Desmond Howarth, Rodney, Alice, Mum and Shaney, Yale Farm, 1956

Southern Rhodesia

The land of milk and honey – Southern Rhodesia; to many people fleeing the war in Europe, it was. It was certainly a beautiful diversified country, as big as Spain, but landlocked. Zambezi Valley in the west, lowveld in the south and the beautiful highlands in the east, Southern Rhodesia had it all.

The climate in general was excellent, usually moderate, with a defined rainy season and no winter to speak of, but it could be really hot in the lowveld, and especially in the Zambezi Valley.

Wild animals in abundance were all that the country was about, and in the Fifties they roamed all over at free will.

Cecil John Rhodes, in his wisdom, claimed this fair land from King Lobengula, for his Queen Victoria of Great Britain in

1894. A remarkable battle took place on the Shangani River in 1893 between Major Allan Wilson with thirty-four men against Lobengula's thousands of warriors. The battle lasted all morning and at eleven o'clock the Matabele called on the surviving white men to surrender; but they had no thought of submission. About noon the last white man died.

The Matabele Induna, looking at the circle of bodies, intoned the words which were remembered with pride in Rhodesia: 'They were men of men,' he said, 'and their fathers were men before them.'

Cecil John Rhodes eventually had their remains moved to World's View in the Matopos, where the founder himself rests. A high school in Salisbury was named Allan Wilson Technical School after the great Major, and Rodney had the privilege of attending and excelled at rugby and business acumen.

Southern Rhodesia is probably best known for the grand, spectacular waterfall about midway along the course of the Zambezi River, at the border between Northern and Southern Rhodesia.

A British explorer, David Livingstone, was the first European to see the Falls and put them 'on the map', naming them Victoria Falls in November 1855, after his English Queen. The explorer's statue still stands on the Southern Rhodesian side.

Approximately twice as wide and twice as deep as the Niagara Falls, the waterfall spans the entire breadth of the Zambezi River at one of its widest points (more than 550 feet). The Falls' mean flow is almost 33,000 cubic feet per second.

The Zambezi River does not gather speed as it nears the drop, the approach being signalled only by the mighty roar and characteristic veil of mist, for which the local Ndebele people named the falls Amanza Thunquayo – the smoke that thunders. This spectacular scene attracts people from all over the world.

Another equally magnificent sight (but manmade) further down the river is the Kariba Dam. Completed in 1959 with a surface area of 5,500 square kilometres, the Kariba Dam is one of the largest manmade lakes in the world, and its installed generation capacity today is 1,300 megawatts.

Kariba soon became a national and international play-ground; the tiger fishing championships are held annually (Dorothy's husband, Desmond, being a willing participant), and the best freshwater fish ever is caught (and cooked in a little bit of butter) there; bream, just heaven's delight.

The dam attracts many wild animals and bird life; Buffalo roam at will, even coming into the camping sites at night.

Kariba Dam was, and always will be, a great asset to both countries on its borders.

The might of the 2,650 kilometre Zambezi River is legendary. It cuts a swathe through Africa from Angola, which borders the Atlantic, to Mozambique on the Indian Ocean, and along it forms the border between landlocked Northern and Southern Rhodesia.

Perhaps the most important and historically interesting site in Southern Rhodesia is Zimbabwe Ruins. The ruins which gave their name to modern Zimbabwe cover some 1,800 acres and are the largest ancient stone constructions south of the Sahara.

The stone-carved Zimbabwe Bird is an emblem of the country, and appears now on the national flag and on the bank notes and coins.

Who built the stone fortress has always been open to controversy. The Portuguese traders who built trading posts right across Africa was one theory. More popular with the local people was that it is their heritage left by their ancestors; but whoever built this impressive fortress has become part of this beautiful country's charm.

As a family in the Fifties, we always thought the Eastern Highlands were the prettiest of places and most accessible.

Inyanga, with its rolling green hills; the capital, Umtali, with its avenues of lilac Jacaranda trees, with the breathtaking heights of the Vumba; and the sheer views across to neighbouring Mozambique are magnificent.

'A land of contrasts, and the inhabitants a race completely without guile,' as Pater said.

Printed in the United States
104076LV00001B/140/A

9 781844 014729